C000253087

KINSHIP

poems by

Maxim D. Shrayer

Finishing Line Press
Georgetown, Kentucky

KINSHIP

Copyright © 2024 by Maxim D. Shrayer
ISBN 979-8-88838-530-2 First Edition
All rights reserved under International and Pan-American Copyright Conventions. No part of this book may be reproduced in any manner whatsoever without written permission from the publisher, except in the case of brief quotations embodied in critical articles and reviews.

Publisher: Leah Huete de Maines
Editor: Christen Kincaid
Cover Art: Maxim D. Shrayer
Author Photo: Lee Pellegrini
Cover Design: Elizabeth Maines McCleavy

Order online: www.finishinglinepress.com
also available on amazon.com

Author inquiries and mail orders:

FinishingBooks@aol.com
(502) 603-0670

Finishing Line Press
PO Box 1626
Georgetown, Kentucky 40324
USA

Contents

for
　　Tatiana
　　　　Mira
　　　　　Karen

Kinship

"Ukraine, my birthland," grandfather Aron (Arkady) used to say.
He grew up in Kamianets-Podilskyi and only in the 1920s
Moved to Moscow. Became a paver, then a telephone engineer.
My other grandfather, Peysakh (Pyotr), was also born in Kamianets.
Prior to entering the gymnasium he spoke Ukrainian not as well
As Yiddish, but still much better than Russian. After a lifetime
Of living in Leningrad, Grandfather Pyotr never forgot Ukraine—
The high bank of the Smotrych, the Turkish bridge, the mills
On the land our family used to rent from a Polish count.

Nyusya Moshkovna Studnits, my maternal grandmother, was born
In the town of Bar, now in Vinnytsia Province. She studied
At the Kharkiv Institute of Engineering and Economics.
In the late 1930s, she married and settled in Moscow
To become a consummate resident of the capital.
She spoke Russian with barely a trace of the Ukrainian accent,
Her speech giving away the old Moscow singsong intonation.
And yet to her—a Jewish woman, a Muscovite—Ukraine remained
The realm of youth and orphanhood, the house of first love.

My mother was born in Moscow, my father, in Leningrad.
As young people they visited with the relatives—who had survived
And returned to Ukraine after the Shoah—in Kamianets, Kyiv,
Vinnytsia, and Odessa. During the twenty years I spent
In the former empire, only once did I visit Ukraine.
Summer of 1986, a brief stay in Luhansk Province … Years later
Already an American, a Jewish immigrant, I came to Kyiv,
First alone, then with my older daughter Mira. She was seven.
Six months later Russia annexed the Crimean Peninsula.

Visiting Ukraine during the post-Soviet years, I was in the grip
Of mixed emotions. Yes, this was the birthplace of my grandparents,
The land in which our family tree was deeply rooted.
In this sense, my experience was typical of Soviet Jews.
Could I think of Ukraine only as a place on a map of the past,
Where generations of my ancestors had been born and raised,

Went to shul, worked the land? How could I not think of Ukraine
As a place on the map of Europe, where in ditches and ravines,
At the bottom of ponds lay our bones—the bones of murdered Jews.

Why speak about it now? Because on February 24,
All those jumbled, contradictory feelings receded
Into the background. Ukraine became my own native land
When the enemies of peace invaded. Now Ukraine
Is a target of Russia's imperial aggression. A victim
With which I feel both kinship and solidarity.
Every day I undergo emotional torment because
The troops of Russia, the land of my first language,
Are massacring Ukraine—to my terror and shame.

As I think of the war in Ukraine, I cannot but turn in my thoughts
To those men and women who wear Russian military uniforms,
And especially to the culpable, the generals and admirals,
The commanding officers of the Russian army, air force, and navy.
If only one of them refused to carry out their orders.
If only one hesitated to turn soldiers into statistics.
If only one of them cared not to disfigure what little remains
Of Russia's culture and its hopes for the future.

Cursed be you, the bedlamite who dispatched the Russian troops
To annihilate Ukraine, to die on my ancestors' native land.

At the Elbow of Cape Cod

Dusk in September
tender, like sealskin,
lilted, like lavender.

Who is your next of kin?
Who—your avenger?
What chafing lexicon

captures your anger?
Whom do you con
into saying your prayer?

Come, slay my dragon,
be my soothsayer.
Dress like a drag queen,

wear red eyeliner.
Maple and oaken
ocean weather,

lipsung and spoken,
loved and forsaken.

The Linguist

for M. J. Connolly

The linguist sees the world
and takes it by the horns,
the linguist loves the word
before the word is born.

The linguist deconstructs
the mystery of sound,
he trusts and yet mistrusts;
he is forever bound.

When worlds fall apart,
when people fail to speak,
the linguist feels a spark.

He knows his sacred place:
by practicing his art
the linguist keeps the peace.

Valse Triste

Dogs in the park maintain the proper distance,
they probably sense the owners' reluctance
to come together and take an open stance
against the powers of happenstance.

The park is like a hospital; with masks on
the people's faces hide their contagion,
yet every walker in the park could be an agent
of the mysterious, virulent invasion.

Some canine partners look quite attractive
in their masks and gloves, hence the protective
attire has become the new elective
affinity, a fashion for the restive.

The weeping willows clench their greening lancets,
to them, of course, the human strife is senseless,
with our dogs, in our silly dresses
we look so incredibly defenseless.

Life in the park is growing distant, static;
we stand apart and talk: an Irish medic,
a Russian immigrant, a German academic.
It's just another day of post-pandemic…

Stronger: For Tatiana

Mein junger Sohn fragt mich: Soll ich Geschichte lernen?
Bertold Brecht

My younger daughter asked me
        while writing a paper on antisemitism:
"The teacher told us to come up
        with arguments against our own theses.
Papa, I'm confused,
        what should I tell him?"

You tell him, I said, there is
        no argument against truth.
Tell him, a thesis in favor of prejudice
        would be an impossible ruse.

Six months later my younger daughter
        asked me, after getting her history syllabus:
"There are many kinds of prejudice here,
        but not a word about Jew-hatred.
I feel like we've been thrown under the bus.
        Papa, what should I say to the teacher?"

Say to her that selective justice
        is a form of bigotry.
You say to her, they cannot hide the evidence—
        no matter how hard they try.

On the eve of her Bat Mitzvah
        I asked my younger daughter:
"Taniusha, how do you feel?"
        She put her hand on my shoulder—
lightly, gently, like my older angel.
        "I'm good, Papa," she answered. "I'm stronger."

Minsk Elegy

for Boris Dralyuk

In the year 1942 my relative Misha Luditsky,
A student, volunteered to fight the Germans.
He deported Chechens and Crimean Tatars.
Never once did he taste of battle. He only witnessed
The inexplicable punishment of nations.
Stalin's victory plan, so perfectly wicked.

In 1945 second lieutenant M. L. returned to the funeral of Minsk,
Eighty thousand Jews. But a handful lived.
He married the daughter of a Jewish butcher
From Komarovka Market and a local party activist,
Daughter of Rabbi Chaim-Wolf, of blessed memory, my great-grandfather.
Thus we were related. Almost everything about it was messed up.

In the early 1960s Misha heard the sermons of the dissident General G.
He planned to join the Union for the Struggle to Restore Lenin's Creed,
Repeated the general's maxim that only rats belonged in the underfloor.
The authorities had a chat with Misha. He lay low, fearing arrest.
Worked in a construction trust. Smoked Bulgarian cigarettes.
Every now and then he would come to Moscow on a shopping spree.

Once I visited Misha and the family in Minsk. The year of the Olympic boycott.
They lived in a cluttered apartment on Avenue Źmitrok Biadula,
Named after the Belarusian nightingale, a Jew from around Vilna.
It was then I felt, for the first time, how time can history backward.
And I realized that life can get around on broken stilts
Of the past. It can barely move yet keeps at it.

And all the while my relative wouldn't leave me alone.
He ambushed me in the living room beside a gramophone
And played a prewar record of a squeaky Yiddish song.
Son, tell me, does this grab your soul?
And all I could think was, you're such an asshole,
As I nodded and trembled with genuine boredom.

Misha sat at the head of the table and gulped brandy from a tea glass.
Spoke about the gang of party thieves and drunks that robbed us
Of everything. Served the spiciest cholent and the sweetest tzimmes.
Eat some more, son. Tell us about yourself. Share your news.
Who do you have besides us? We're all that's left of the mishpocha...
And that's what I remember about the Minsk vacation.

In the year 1991 they moved to Israel. O merciless Lethe.
I could never find them. The finest of repatriates' rivers...
So many years have passed, it seems like it never happened.
Only a long drive back, the tallow end of summer in Belarus.
Only buckets full of purple plums left on the roadside,
Scabs of memory on the body of the murdered shtetlach.

Apples 'n Honey

Apples 'n Honey, Apples 'n Honey,
that's a Jewish New Year's ghost.
They appear in a hurry
aiding those who ache the most.

They are both masked and maskless,
vaccinated and exempt,
they remind us of countless
apple orchards left unspent.

They are sweet and also sour,
like a shtetl's main street.
They evoke clouds of flour
and the burning smell of peat.

Apples 'n Honey, Apples 'n Honey,
jars of amber, broken crate…
Don't count your restless money,
hide your tears and celebrate.

L'Éducation Sentimentale

Soviet women past their prime
in aubergine turtlenecks washed to a sheen,
Vera Josephovna Pearlbaum,
Lubov Leonidovna Burnstein.

Public detractors of Stalin,
secret admirers of Pasternak,
keepers of old family cooking styles,
cloves and garlic, celery and parsnip.

"Dear children, you must love the classics,"
they preached in voices laced with pain
as our masters shot down a South Korean liner
west of Sakhalin in the Sea of Japan.

"The English teacher, she's no dummy," spoke one classmate.
"Jews are usually smart." I stared out the window.
"Fucking Russian teacher," spoke another classmate.
"The sniveling Jewbitch." I smashed the window.

"All the world's a stage, and we're merely players,"
repeated Vera Williamovna Pearstein.
"Children, drop by drop, squeeze out the slave,"
repeated Lubov Antonovna Burnbaum.

Outside the window the warmhearted playboy Brezhnev was dying,
after him the bloodthirsty spymaster Andropov was dying,
after him the timid party secretary Chernenko was dying,
then Gorbachev fought for his spot under the sun of the dying.

We read "Lady with Lapdog," we memorized Shakespeare's sonnets,
we learned to love and betray one another.
A whole lifetime wouldn't be enough
to shake the memories of this rancorous theater.

Bilateral Pneumonia

They put him right near the entrance,
The rooms on the floor were full up.
Boris Pasternak

In a crowded hospital room
my father was fighting pneumonia,
both hands guarded him from
doctors and stinging needles.

His roommate, a tram operator,
by the name of "Montgomery, James,"
was a classic Bostonian; a joker.
Now he slept like a corpse.

A stream of visitors—grandkids,
nephews, brothers, and sons—
flowed in to hug James' blanket,
begged him to outwit death.

My father dozed off, his Chaldean eyes
striking the metal window pane
where began the environs of paradise;
he and I walked there alone.

The landscape outside the window
smoked like a winter playground;
chimney over the parsonage, willow,
careening black dog, the merry fool.

I was trying my best to urge the syllables
as if praying for a son or daughter,
or for a healing downpour
to fall on the empty fields.

A Russian-American Novel

for K.

You played the cello at a classmate's wedding...
It was a hot September in Vermont
many years ago. The girls had not been born
though we were trying. Desperately? Not
so much, not yet—the happy ending
obliterates the memory of want.

You played the cello in a sage green outfit,
sleeves flowing on the mountain air.
I don't remember what you played. Glière?
Or was it Bruch? Some long-forgotten tier
of melodies, a hideaway, an orbit
where hours were long, arms bare.

You played the cello, but it was your old cello,
the one the cleaners dropped and cracked.
An accident. It had to be replaced.
We bought a German make, it played
so lustrously that we abandoned the yellow
old maple body though we kept the strings...

The married classmate is no longer a kindred spirit,
though once a month you see her at grand rounds.
Our daughters now make their own daily rounds,
replete with teenage sites and sounds,
and only rarely do you and I revisit
the places where the past rebounds.

In those memories you play and smile faintly,
your fingers stir like pebbles in the brook,
your bow unlocks the long-forgotten songbook
in which we lived, allowing for the daily
Tolstoyan miracle, the promise of a family,
Five years. Sixty months. All it took.

The Speaker's Departure

Say, desert geometer, shaper
Of Arabic sand into form...
      Osip Mandelstam

What happened to Speaker Pelosi,
once known for her principled views?
She chose to do what was easy,
she wasn't defending her pews.
I don't really care about
the plausible cause of her strife,
she washes her silence in doubt
and laps up her fear of life.

Three Incarnations of a Moscow Childhood Dachshund

The first one, marten-sleek,
        locked her ancient eyes
                with my pregnant wife
      in a crowded pet store
on the Upper East Side.

The second, blazing red
        like a she-fox at sunset,
                was prepared to tolerate
      her given name of a Greek
goddess of harvest.

The third, a dogscape of dapple,
        raised small clouds of dust
                at a windblown parking lot
      while her Yankee family consumed
their ice cream sundaes.

The Bombing of Odessa

O Russia, my birthland, I pity your destiny…
Russian troops are bombing Odessa.

Putin's generals, death and deputy,
craving Odessa, a fallen Odessa.

As desperate missiles descend on Odessa
poets and sages come to its rescue.

They summon the shadows of fellow singers
who once lived and loved in this city of cities.

They wrote in Yiddish, Ukrainian, Russian,
Hebrew and Polish, Tatar and Italian.

From verses of the past they are rising like zealots
not to allow the murder of Odessa.

Bialik is counting the wounded and the dead, now
the city of slaughter is here, in Odessa.

Akhmatova, lithe like a Black Sea deity,
unsheathes her father's damascus naval dagger.

Simon Frug, the Jewish Aeolian harpist
thrusts a stick hand grenade under his belt.

Sasha Chorny, the scion of Odessan pharmacists
is preparing bottles of anti-tank cocktails.

Jabo, fiercely smiling, like a conjuror at play,
commands a unit of harbor patrol.

Lesia Ukrainka, Khadjibey's salty air,
takes an old shotgun from the dacha's dusty attic.

Bunin trades in his ornate walking stick
for a Mauser rifle with a sword bayonet.

Volodymyr Sosiura mounts a Maxim gun
on the dome of the Opera House at dawn.

Febrile Bagritsky, from Deribasovka's roofs
sends postal doves to Ukrainian troops.

Their voices and weapons form a sound defense
to deter Russia's weapons of death.

Undefeatable and ambidextrous,
we shall always fight for you, my Odessa.

For My Daughters, on Yom Kippur

If there weren't any offenses,
How would neighbors mend their fences?
If we didn't have to fast,
Life would be so fast.

If one's actions weren't demeaning,
Would remorse have meaning?
Being forced to earn forgiveness
Denigrates what hope it gives us.

The Book of Life has lots of room:
Bride is hurrying to her groom,
Wife to husband, babe to mother,
Knife to calf and scythe to mower….

Let us pause on Yom Kippur:
Easy fast and sweet New Year.

Immigrant Quatrains of Clarity

Wind finds the northwest gap, fall comes.
Robert Penn Warren

Melancholy

These are the last treasures
of a New England farmer,
one doesn't get much farther
from summer pleasures.

Appropriation

A Cossack wearing a cassock
at once repulses and delights.
Is he a Boston Red Sox fan?
Does he support abortion rights?

Valediction

Canada geese, thirteen of them, formation
of friends and lovers, ready for migration
to warmer places, where COVID-19 is raging.
Farewell. Fly safe, my secret agents.

Comeuppance

He ruled with dictatorial pride,
decreed with cruel vanity.
Now he must be expressly tried
for crimes against humanity.

Scallopville

Where one-room cottages
once dotted the jagged estuary,
McMansions now hang like vultures
over the coast in January.

Anthropology

A neighbor in a bicycle helmet
is chopping wood in his front yard.
In Russia they would call an ambulance
and take him straight to Ward No. 6.

Gift

The last, parting gift of autumn.
What did I do to deserve such beauty?
On this November day, under the setting sun,
in my hands the heart of winter is beating.

Boston

Father and daughter, masked,
riding the T, post-COVID.
Who could have asked
for a happier moment?

Bats at Sunset

The monster is rotund, vile, enormous, one-hundred-muzzled, and barking.
Aleksandr Radishchev, *after* Vasily Trediakovsky, after Virgil

The woods are lovely, dark and deep...
Robert Frost

Last night the bats were flying so low
that I could see their faces. Each outline
looked like a Soviet relative of mine,
reincarnated in the sunset's afterglow.

One bat resembled mother's Auntie Roza.
She taught the factory lads how to use
the Russian language, that métier of Jews,
who thought they could survive like Russians.

Another had the likeness of Auntie Manya,
my father's aunt who lived and died in Minsk.
She loved extensive stays in Moscow clinics
and never missed a single day of *Pravda*.

At sunset bats are ugly, soft, and fast—
like old snapshots of the Soviet past.

Madness

People you once knew the way the aorta knows its blood
        have suddenly started believing (or pretending to believe)
the despicable lies of Putin's regime.

Do what? Disown them? Argue, mouth-foamed?
        Unfriend in a frenzy? Play a melody plaintive?
Or act as if you're waking up from a bad dream?

My Talented Aunt and Her Political Allegiances

My talented aunt, a musician by trade,
      a Muscovite by origin,
      and a Soviet by breeding,
      took my older daughter for an evening stroll
      to the graveyard, where some of the Kennedys rest,
and delivered this passionate tirade:

"In Russia, where we hail from,
      there was once a terrible Civil War
      between the Reds and the Whites.
      The Reds only wanted to destroy,
      the Whites were what we called the 'white bone'—
the intelligentsia of the nation."

My daughter described how my talented aunt
      explained the meaning of the word "intelligentsia":
      "On January 6th the Whites were the ones
      who went to the Capitol to defend our freedom,
      our culture, and our great values
from today's Reds who were on assault."

What to say about my mother's own sister,
      my grandparents' beloved daughter,
      my very talented aunt?
      The rope was taut. I was choking with anger,
      but instead of another tirade
I pulled out my phone and scrolled through some pictures.

Members of the American intelligentsia:
      the one with a Viking hat and black horns,
      the one in the "Camp Auschwitz" sweatshirt,
      the one who pissed on the floor of the Capitol building,
      and the one who nabbed the speaker's podium.
All of them heroes, the white bones of our nation.

Estonia. Many Years Hence...

My dear Baltic waves have conspired
to take me and carry away
where peeling park benches are tired
of keeping the secrets at bay.

Here charcoal and train station longing
embitter the air of the town;
the jetties run northward, prolonging
the beach and the braided skyline.

We guzzled Estonian beer
and feasted on local fare,
and effortlessly, without ire
I mentioned the Russian warfare.

"You sound like a frontline reporter,"
Maxim said to me. "That's so plain.
Your poems are simpler and shorter,
your essays spell conflict and pain."

And Katya was stubbornly silent
while stirring the thin amber slice
of sunset. She hadn't lost her talent
for noticing artifice.

We knew that this wasn't on purpose,
we felt it within our hearts,
yet saying those words was hurtful.
We're different. Different. But how?

Our dear Baltic waves left us orphaned
yet brought us the old salt taste
of our Soviet childhood...
How can we be saved from ourselves?

Eretz Yisrael: Seven Poems

1. Eden

My father's first cousin,
the octogenarian artist
born in the British Mandate
of Palestine during the best
year of Stalin's terror
and named after the psalmist king—
same as my own father,
who was born in Leningrad—
took us around his childhood
streets and told us:

"Right here on Rothschild Boulevard
on this sunlit bench
Doda Feiga used to take her naps,
the wise old lady from Kamianets.
We would run by and kick the cane
from under her feet
and triumphantly ululating
head over to the sea.
Just south of here lies Neve Tzedek,
where all of Tel Aviv started.

"See that fence and the old carcass
at the corner of Lilienblum and Pines Streets—
the former Eden Cinema.
After the war nearly every week
my parents dragged me
to screenings of Soviet movies.
They watched stories about soldiers
coming home from the war, remembered
The Novorossiysk anchored at the Odessa harbor,
and wept under the yellow stars of the East."

2. Old Train Station

A choo-choo train used to pull the cars
from Jaffa to Jerusalem…
After the terminus was closed in 1948,
the rusty rails were beaten
into ploughshares and pruning hooks.
HaTachana is now an emporium
of souvenir shops, cafés, boutiques,
a retail space of distant memories…

That morning, while standing in the back alley
of Gesher Theater's rehearsal space,
where Russian actors used to memorize their parts
as if they were learning the Hebrew prayers,
I remembered actor Valentin Nikulin
as the Austrian Prince von Berg—
admirer of young male Jewish flautists—
in Arthur Miller's play…

Spring of 1987 at Moscow's Clean Ponds,
Marlen Khutsiev's production,
resurrected by Igor Kvasha
exactly twenty years after it was banned.

The Russian actor Nikulin tossing *Hände weg*
in the face of a Nazi-Communist-Fascist,
Hands off, scum of all times and nations.
The Russian Jew Nikulin,
shrouded in a white shirt,
telling my parents and me as we stood
in the proscenium of a new life,
My dears may G-d protect you.

The Russian *olim* Nikulin who
couldn't find a home for himself
in the Holy Land and returned
to Moscow for his death.

3. Artists' Quarter in Old Jaffa

The frowned forehead of Kikar Kdumim,
a stoneware door sign "Sharir—שריר".
(This used to be the home of our cousins,
such were the rules of that translingual game,
in Israel they Hebraized our name.)

Here lived the artist and his family…
The new owners, a Jewish lady
from Germany and her German husband
destroyed the family abode of harmony
to build their own retirement home.

From here one can see
St. Nicholas Monastery, the Nunciature,
the Al-Bahr Mosque, where fishermen's wives
prayed for their husbands,
and also a majestic restaurant, A-la-din.

Below, warehouses and fishing boats,
and further down—beaches, promenade, hotels,
volleyballs, submachine guns, hips, lips, and heels,
the joys and torments of every Jewish day
imprinted on the sky of Tel Aviv.

4. Shuk HaPishpeshim (Flea Market)

Father and son, distinguished Hasids,
owners of an antiquarian shop,
they offer samovars and kerosene lamps,
mezuzahs, tiles, rusty scythes....
The only things you won't find here
are Russian rhymes and horseshoes.

5. Batya Kahana's Disappearance

Batya Kahana, my paternal
grandfather's first cousin,
even back in Kamianets
composed Russian stories.

Then she married her first cousin—
same relation to my grandfather—
an agent of the insurance firm "Zion,"
who did well for himself in the Mandate
and was prepared to pay fellow expatriates
from the Russian Empire
for translating his wife's work into Hebrew.

According to family lore
after her husband's death she grew silent,
stopped speaking Russian
and never composed again.

In the city of Tel Aviv, on Ben Zakai Street,
in the attic of a two-story villa
built in the middle 1920s,
amid baby strollers and gramophones

I will find a box with Batya Kahana's papers
and finally read
her Russian fictions in the original.

6. Rechavia

Wake up in Jerusalem
Like a babe in her mother's lap.
Unshut your eyes and see:
You're in the room of a traveler's inn,
sleeping next to you on a narrow cot
your own—G-d's—creation,
an eight-year-old daughter.
And all the metaphors mix
on the palette of Saturday morning.

7. Wailing Wall

In a black ankle-length skirt,
purchased in Mea She'arim
in a girls' clothing basement,

a white band on her brow
a white cloud on the blue sky
draped over Jerusalem,

my younger daughter,
Tatiana Rebecca,
accompanied me to the Kotel.

When we reached the boundary
where men and boys turn to the north
and women and girls, to the south,

I'm scared to go alone, my daughter said,
and I led her—a girl a boy a butterfly—
where the pilgrims flowed.

We forded the crowd, found a crevice
between the time-molten stones,
and inserted our notes in two languages:

....
....

The Salt Pond in Autumn

for Mira

The season's last butterflies
in near-death delirium
dance like schoolgirls
dotting the shoreline,
dropping radiance
from dainty pinafores,
G-d is granting
the death of pine forests.

Why do you frown
my dearest pilgrim?
Waves of the Danube,
the waltz of immigrants
briny Slavic lyrics
Jewish notes played too fast,
American imperatives
to obliterate the past.

We've forgotten it all,
we couldn't forget,
howling like a whale
beached at Nantucket.
We pressed the lemon of memories
squeezed it inside out;
the highball of reveries,
the lowball of time.

Crimean Sonnet

for Andrew Sofer

I don't recall the outbreak, just the panic:
August of 1970, Sebastopol, the smell
of rotting apricots, my mother's dainty tunic,
Uchkuevka beach, the heat, the groundswell

of fear. Seething lines at ticket office,
vacationers like war evacuees.
The talk of cholera. Words like "orifice"
or "dehydration" hanging in the breeze.

The hasty packing. My collection of stag beetles
forgotten on the windowsill. Our train
arriving at Kursk Station. Empty bottles.
My parents kissing on the platform. Reunion.

I didn't know another parting was near:
my father, a doctor, would be dispatched to Crimea.

Tired

a Jew
is
tired
of
love unrequited

a Jew
is
tired
of
being weird

a Jew
is
tired
of
feeling admired

a Jew
is
tired
of
benevolent tyrants

a Jew
is
tired
of
waiting for the Messiah

a Jew is
a Jew is   a Jew is
tired
a Jew is   a Jew is
a Jew is

Homecoming

On the eve of his birthday, in April, the Composer can't sleep…
Unforgivable insomnia, he'll say to his wife in the morning.
Coffee, strong. Cream-infused. Empty rooms like a glaring chessboard.
Fearless games of lawn tennis, domain of the young. Checkered jacket.
Dainty Florentine pencil. A blank index card. Right to left
The Composer scribbles: *Isaiah… And thus He shall judge among nations.*

Now Véra has closed her eyes in the bedroom. He knows it's time
To depart as the memories rise from the African drylands.
Navy jacket, full zip. Knee high socks. Pleated shorts. Newsboy cap.
Pocket sepulchers for butterflies. *My son has a rich velvet voice.*
Will my coffin be draped with black velvet? The burning Arabian sands.
I will not visit Germany, no. I won't ever go back to Russia.

The Composer walks on the lakefront. A castle looms ahead.
Young Tolstoy followed comely Swiss maids in the holiday crowd.
On the other side, showing white through the purple nightfall,
Mountain peaks in white astrakhans. Fur coats of teetering skies.
His direction—south-west. There—a mountain pass.
And beyond—after Marcus Aurelius—cometh the hour of parting. . .

Distant shores of America, whaling harpoon of Cape Cod,
Where the brooding Composer spent Easter holiday alone.
It was March '42. He was writing an émigré tale
The New Yorker had asked for. How madly he wanted to bring
His abandoned protagonist back from a British dominion
And to send him to Libya against Rommel's Afrika Korps.

College town with a name so Homeric, but hardly a laugh.
How they lived for a decade surrounded by provincial languor?
Sprawling campus. The library. Lectures. Dactylic weekends.
It was here he finally managed to wake up with fame on his lips.
What remains of his presence? And what of his teaching? A plaque?
Here Professor Such-and-Such wrote his greatest American works.

The Composer walks down the hill. His next stop: Highland Road.
Here they lived in three different houses, each populated by ghosts.
In that Tudor a wistful nymphet filled his pages with tainted love.
Down the street there's a cottage. Pale fire illumines its ceilings.
And that redbrick colonial—what a magnificent attic!
There he left his America. Exile's immobile baggage...

The Composer stands on a slippery dock at the tip of Manhattan.
He can see Ellis Island. It's closed to immigrant traffic.
How long has it been since the boatsful of refugees arrived?
How long has it been? Europe. Nazism. The war. The escape.
He remembers Grunewald… how they stood on the old bridge that night.
How they strolled in Charlottenburg, giddy with love and oblivion.

However many times did the Germans invite him—he always wrote back.
He was ready to come to Berlin as a passionate denouncer.
But it's now too late to condemn their crimes. And to France?
Well, in Paris his friends are no more. Khodasevich is gone.
Charming Mark Aleksandrych Aldanov is gone. Bitter Bunin is gone.
No rivals. No old Russian flames. They've all since departed.

Beach in Cannes. Cinema. The Composer stands by the edge
Of the water. He hears the calls of muezzins at dawn.
It is time for the righteous to perform Fajr Salah. But here?
Mosques in Cannes? Why? He suddenly thinks of his youth in Crimea.
Their trip to the palace of the Khans... No ship can transport him
Past the radiant Bosporus—across the Black Sea and to Yalta.

Stubborn rumors still making the rounds: he came to the USSR
In disguise, as a Protestant minister from rural New Hampshire.
That in Leningrad he stood near his parents' elegant mansion
Just two blocks from St. Isaac's Cathedral. And later he wept
At the site of their former estate on the Oredezh River.
Never happened. So don't believe those forgers of legends.

Though he swore he would never return, history has compelled
Him to leap over the Baltic when drawbridges drop their arms.
The Composer sees rostral columns and stone-clad mermaids.
Lachrymarum… But sudden salt tears have dried on his eyes.
He's in Russia not to cry but to wrest from the cannibals' hands
What is left of his body. He hurries, the sunrise approaching.

Who gave those Communazi descendants the right
To adorn their dirty red aprons with his noble last name?
Manuscripts, books with drawings, his family photographs
Trapped in airless vaults of the former Department of Customs.
Just as he never once acquiesced to the rule of the looters,
His possessions refuse to discredit the Composer's authorial will.

The Composer ascends the dark staircase up to the floor
Where cabinets are stuffed with the stolen émigré letters.
Empty shipping containers bear witness to theft and disgrace.
I will never submit. I will never surrender.
The Composer fashions his r's so brightly. His elderly cadence majestic.
Murderers, curse on you! I'm taking what's rightfully mine.

All the papers eventually turn to dust. Even family treasures—
To the junkyard of history... The Composer favors a different plan.
No wonder the clever ratcatcher from Hamelin has been on his mind.
Yet this time all the rats will remain. Books will also remain.
Only words will follow him, leaving behind empty pages
To the city of the plague which was once the Composer's home.

It's all over. Mercury, Neptune, and Ceres
See him off with a copper-lipped fare-thee-well and forgive us.
Lions, gryphons, and sphinxes stand guard on the granite embankment.
The Bronze Horseman rides off. On the Neva the steamboat groans.
The Composer is leaving. He will never return to his homeland...
Lake Geneva is quiet. White swans gently glide on the water.

Acknowledgments

This book would not exist, either in its Russian and Jewish origins or in its Anglo-American shape, were it not for my father, David Shrayer-Petrov, who taught me poetry, and my mother, Emilia Shrayer, who taught me English. Thank you, *papochka* and *mamochka*.

And this book would never have been composed without the love and support of my wife, Karen E. Lasser, and our daughters, Tatiana Rebecca Shrayer and Mira Isabella Shrayer, all of whom understand poetry in different ways. Finally, the anapestic barks of Stella are in many of the book's cadences.

Previous incarnations of four poems in this book originally appeared in *Of Politics and Pandemics: Songs of a Russian Immigrant*. Earlier versions of some of the poems included in this collection were first published in the following journal and magazines: *On the Seawall, Minyan, Northern Appalachia Review, The Raven's Perch, ROAR (Russian Oppositional Arts Review), Society of Classical Poets, The Blue Mountain Review,* and *Vita Poetica*. The poem "My Talented Aunt and Her Political Allegiances" won 2nd place in the 2022 Humans of the World Winter Poetry Contest. I would like to thank the editors and staff for having given e-space and print-space to my work.

I'm deeply grateful to the poets Boris Dralyuk, Elizabeth Poliner, and Andrew Sofer for their friendship and their generous and insightful comments on some of the poems in this book.

Dobrochna Fire edited the manuscript with tolerance for the translingual author's imperfect pitch.

Last but not least, I would like to thank Leah Huete de Maines and the entire editorial and production team at Finishing Line Press for giving this book a hospitable home.

Maxim D. Shrayer, bilingual author, scholar, and translator, was born in Moscow in 1967 to a Jewish-Russian family with Ukrainian and Lithuanian roots and spent over eight years as a refusenik. He and his parents, the writer David Shrayer-Petrov and the translator Emilia Shrayer, left the USSR and immigrated to the United States in 1987. Shrayer received a PhD from Yale University in 1995. He is a professor at Boston College, where he cofounded the Jewish Studies Program. Shrayer has authored and edited more than twenty-five books of nonfiction, criticism, fiction, poetry, and translations. His poetry collections include the Russian-language *Tabun nad lugom* (*Herd above the Meadow*, New York, 1990), *Amerikanskii romans* (*American Romance*, Moscow, 1994), *N'iukheivenskie sonety* (*New Haven Sonnets*, Providence, 1998), and *Stikhi iz aipada* (*Poems from the iPad*, Tel Aviv, 2022), and the English-language *Of Politics and Pandemics* (Boston, 2020). Among Shrayer's other books are the literary memoirs *Waiting for America, Leaving Russia*, and *Immigrant Baggage* and the collections of fiction *Yom Kippur in Amsterdam* and *A Russian Immigrant: Three Novellas*. He is the recipient of a number of awards and fellowships, including a 2007 National Jewish Book Award and a 2012 Guggenheim Fellowship. Shrayer's publications have been translated into eleven languages, most recently *Nabokov e o Judaísmo*, published in Brazil in 2023, and *Immigrato russo*, published in Italy in 2024. He lives in Massachusetts with his wife, Dr. Karen E. Lasser, a medical researcher and physician, their daughters, Mira Isabella and Tatiana Rebecca, and their silver Jewdle, Stella.

Milton Keynes UK
Ingram Content Group UK Ltd.
UKHW020314060424
440664UK00003B/34

9 798888 385302